GW01255667

Original title:

The Silent Woods

Author: Eliora Lumiste

ISBN HARDBACK: 978-9916-79-672-6

ISBN PAPERBACK: 978-9916-79-673-3

ISBN EBOOK: 978-9916-79-674-0

Silence Engraved in Nature's Frame

In the woods where whispers dwell,
The rustling leaves weave tales to tell.
Soft shadows dance on the ground below,
As cool winds hum a gentle flow.

Amidst the trees, a stillness reigns,
Nature's heartbeat, free from chains.
The brook babbles secrets to the stone,
In this serene world, I feel at home.

Mountains loom with silent grace,
Kissing the sky, a timeless embrace.
Clouds drift lightly, dreams in their wake,
In this quiet moment, hearts awake.

Moonlight spills on the silent lake,
A mirror of peace that night did make.
Stars twinkle softly, a distant choir,
Each note a wish, each breath a fire.

Here in nature's gentle sway,
Silence speaks in its own way.
With every sigh, every rustle,
The soul finds strength in the hustle.

Journey Through the Veil of Calm

Pages turn in gentle breeze,
Softly sung by whispering trees.
Paths unfold like silken dreams,
Where light dances by the streams.

Footsteps trace the silent ground,
In this peace, solace is found.
Time drifts slow, like clouds above,
Wrapped in warmth, we feel the love.

Each moment glows, a fleeting spark,
Guiding us through the veiled dark.
Hearts align with nature's call,
In this journey, we stand tall.

Floating thoughts, like petals glide,
In the calm where dreams abide.
Magic lingers in the air,
A gentle peace beyond compare.

As we wander, truths unwind,
In this space, our souls aligned.
Together here, no fear can reign,
Journey onward, free from pain.

Whispers in the Thicket

In tangled vines, secrets weave,
Amidst the leaves, where shadows breathe.
Voices echo, soft and low,
In this thicket, wisdom flows.

Sunlight glints through emerald hues,
Carrying with it tales to choose.
Nature sings a haunting song,
In the thicket, we belong.

Every rustle, every sigh,
Holds a truth that cannot die.
Listening close, we hear the past,
Whispers linger, shadows cast.

In mossy beds, memories lay,
Guiding us along the way.
Beneath branches, time stands still,
In this thicket, hearts can fill.

With each step, the forest breathes,
Life's unfolding tapestry weaves.
In nature's hush, we hear the calls,
Whispers dance as twilight falls.

Echoes Beneath the Canopy

Softly humming, winds will play,
Underneath the leaves, they sway.
Echoes linger, calls of yore,
In the canopy, dreams explore.

Each rustle tells a tale untold,
In this embrace, we find the bold.
Shadows stretch as daylight wanes,
Echoes pulse through grassy lanes.

Every moment, nature's hymn,
Calls us back when chances skim.
Underneath this leafy dome,
In the echoes, we find home.

With every footfall, stories rise,
Beneath the vast and open skies.
Hearts entwined, we walk as one,
As echoes dance with setting sun.

Time drips down like morning dew,
In the canopy, thoughts renew.
Lost in reverie's calm embrace,
Echoes linger, time and space.

Shadows of the Unheard

In silenced corners, shadows creep,
Voices linger but seldom speak.
Hidden truths in twilight's clutch,
Shadows beckon, softening touch.

Faintly brushed by midnight's veil,
Tales unfold in whispers frail.
Unseen journeys intertwine,
In the quiet, peace divine.

Every heartbeat, every sigh,
Holds the weight of days gone by.
In shadows deep, we find our art,
Unheard voices, a tender heart.

Through forgotten paths and dreams,
Shadows dance in moonlit beams.
Carrying the whispers near,
Hushed confessions, crystal clear.

In stillness, stories start to glow,
Shadows of the unheard flow.
With each step, we break the chains,
In the silence, life remains.

Hushed Conversations of Flora and Fauna

Soft whispers dance in the breeze,
Leaves rustle in joyful tease.
Flowers nod in gentle sway,
Nature speaks in its own way.

Crickets chirp under the moon,
Their chorus sings a sweet tune.
Beneath the stars, a secret shared,
In stillness, all is bared.

The brook babbles with delight,
Reflecting calm through the night.
Petals blush in twilight's glow,
In this hush, all feelings flow.

Branches lean, a tender bow,
Time holds its breath, here and now.
The air is thick with stories untold,
In patterns woven, life unfolds.

In the hush, we come alive,
With every sound, we learn to thrive.
Fauna and flora intertwine,
In the silence, we define.

Moments in the Lush Embrace

In the forest's gentle fold,
Stories of old are softly told.
Sunlight filters through the leaves,
Caressing all that nature weaves.

Moss carpets the ancient ground,
Each step a whisper, a secret found.
Birds flit by on splintered wings,
Singing of joys that summer brings.

A breeze carries scents anew,
Each breath a gift, each shade a clue.
Beneath the boughs, where shadows rest,
Life nestles close, forever blessed.

In every corner, magic hides,
With faithful trees as timeless guides.
The world breathes deep in vibrant hues,
Moments captured, like morning dews.

As day surrenders to night's embrace,
Stars flicker in the vast expanse.
In silence wrapped, we find our place,
In every moment, love's sweet trace.

Through the Thickets of Silence

Twilight cloaks the whispering trees,
Shadows dance in the cooling breeze.
Paths unknown twist and turn,
In the quiet, secrets burn.

Leaves brush softly like a sigh,
Underneath the endless sky.
Gentle echoes of the night,
Guide us home with silver light.

The stillness thick with dreams untold,
Annealing warmth against the cold.
Each footfall a song of the heart,
Through the thickets, we drift apart.

Moonbeams lace the quiet ground,
In this moment, peace is found.
The world pauses, time stands still,
In silence, all expressions thrill.

Through the dark, our spirits soar,
Finding solace, wanting more.
In the thickets, we belong,
In the silence, we grow strong.

The Tapestry of Stillness Unfolds

Threads of dawn weave through the day,
Color and texture in soft array.
Each moment stitched in quiet grace,
Patterns formed in nature's embrace.

The air holds stories, rich and deep,
Where shadows linger, secrets keep.
Time glides slow, like silk unspooled,
In this silence, we are ruled.

Petals open, a soft reveal,
The heart's rhythm, a gentle feel.
With each breath, the world expands,
In quietude, we understand.

Stillness weaves a tapestry bright,
A canvas painted with pure light.
Each thread a tale under the sun,
In the hush, all becomes one.

As twilight dances and stars ignite,
We find warmth in the cool of night.
In the tapestry of life, behold,
The stories of us, beautifully told.

Tranquil Footfalls in the Forest Dreaming

Gentle whispers weave through trees,
Soft shadows dance upon the leaves.
Each step a note in nature's song,
As echoes fade, the heart feels strong.

Birds flit by in joyous flight,
Sunlight filters, pure and bright.
With every breath, the world slows down,
In this embrace, peace can be found.

Moss carpets paths where secrets lie,
Rustling ferns beneath the sky.
The rhythm lulls, a sacred trance,
In forest depths, the soul's romance.

Beneath a bough where dreams take form,
The heart aligns with nature's norm.
In tranquil footfalls, worries cease,
A whispering sigh, a moment's peace.

Among the roots and winding trails,
The forest breathes, and darkness pales.
With every step, the spirit roams,
In tranquil footfalls, the heart finds home.

Capturing the Quiet Song of Nature

In stillness rests the morning dew,
Soft notes arise in whispers true.
Each leaf sways with a gentle grace,
A quiet song in nature's space.

The brook babbles a soothing rhyme,
Lulling hearts in perfect time.
Crickets chirp their nightly tune,
Underneath the watchful moon.

Colors shift as daylight fades,
In twilight's grasp, the silence wades.
Stars awaken, a million eyes,
In harmony with boundless skies.

Reflective ponds hold secrets deep,
Nature's heart in silence keeps.
With every breath, we find our way,
To capture peace at close of day.

In every rustle, every sigh,
A symphony where spirits fly.
Nature's song, both pure and bright,
Guides our souls through dark and light.

The Unseen Watcher in the Green

Amidst the leaves, a presence stays,
A silent guide through tangled ways.
The unseen watcher, wise and old,
In every shadow, stories told.

Branches sway as if to greet,
Ancient secrets at our feet.
In tranquil skies and rustling trees,
The watcher breathes with every breeze.

Eyes that see but never glance,
Witnessing life's fleeting dance.
With hidden roots and steadfast ground,
In nature's heart, life's pulse is found.

The songs of birds, a soft delight,
Echo the watcher's steadfast light.
In whispered winds, we come to know,
The unseen watcher watches slow.

In every rustle, every sound,
The gentle watcher can be found.
Cradled in green, our spirits lift,
As nature's love becomes our gift.

Spaces Where Light Bends

In twilight hours, the world transforms,
Where light and shadow weave their forms.
A golden glow meets silken shade,
In spaces where the light has played.

Through canopies of verdant hues,
A gentle kiss of sunlit cues.
Each ray a brush that paints the ground,
In harmony, the silence found.

Reflecting pools where moments sift,
Capture glimmers, nature's gift.
Every corner hints of grace,
In the dance of time and space.

Whispers ride on every breeze,
As joy awakens in the trees.
In spirals where the light descends,
We find our breath where magic blends.

In every pause, the world expands,
Embracing dreams with open hands.
Where light bends low and shadows bend,
We find the path that will not end.

Beneath the Boughs of Reflection

In the stillness of dusk, I find,
Shadows dance softly, entwined.
Whispers of memories gently thread,
Beneath the boughs, where dreams are led.

A mirror of wishes, the water flows,
Carrying echoes of long-lost prose.
Time in the forest drifts like a song,
In this embrace, where I belong.

Leaves rustle secrets, softly spun,
Under the charm of the setting sun.
Nature cradles, with arms so wide,
Beneath the boughs, my heart confides.

Glimmers of twilight flicker and fade,
Beneath the shelter where hopes cascade.
Moments suspended, like stars in the night,
Here in the hush, all feels just right.

Quiet reflections, a gentle tide,
Memories linger, no need to hide.
Under the branches, life slows its pace,
Beneath the boughs, I find my place.

Secrets Held by the Elder Trees

Ancient sentinels, wise and grand,
Guarding the tales of this sacred land.
Bark like pages, stories unfold,
Secrets held in roots, strong and bold.

Whispers of ages drift in the breeze,
Carried softly through swaying leaves.
In every knot and every knot's tale,
Lies a legacy that will prevail.

Sunlight dapples the forest floor,
In shadows deep, legends roar.
Elder trees stand, firm and proud,
Voices of nature, echoing loud.

In the silence, a knowing glance,
Life's fragile dance, a timeless romance.
Through rustling canopies, truth is spun,
In their presence, we are all one.

Secrets cherished, in silence bequeathed,
Life's tapestry woven, though often wreathed.
Each ring a chapter, each leaf a page,
Elder trees whisper to all of age.

The Soft Breath of the Earth

Morning dew kisses the waking grass,
Nature stirs gently, moments pass.
A whisper of life in every green hue,
The soft breath of Earth, forever true.

Mountains rise high, touching the sky,
Birds soar above as clouds drift by.
In every crevice, in every seam,
Lies the heart of a silent dream.

Rivers hum softly, flowing with grace,
Echoing secrets of time and space.
Under the surface, life thrives and plays,
In the soft breath of Earth, the spirit sways.

A wildflower sways with delicate ease,
Beckoning travelers, carried by breeze.
In every heartbeat, a rhythm we share,
The soft breath of Earth, a loving prayer.

From valleys deep to the heights of light,
In the arms of the Earth, we take flight.
With each dawning day, a chance to renew,
In the soft breath of Earth, we find our view.

Woven Silence in Woodlands

In the heart of the woods, silence weaves,
Threads of tranquility in gentle leaves.
A tapestry rich with stories untold,
Woven silence, a balm for the bold.

Footsteps are hushed on the soft, mossy ground,
In this sacred space, no chaos is found.
Nature's own lullaby, soft and low,
Woven silence where whispers grow.

Branches embrace, like arms spread wide,
In this quiet realm, the world can hide.
The rustle of leaves, a serene refrain,
Woven silence in woodlands remains.

Moonlight filters through, a silver lace,
In the stillness, we find our place.
With every heartbeat, the night does call,
In woven silence, we lose and find all.

Retreat to the woods, where calmness resides,
In the embrace of the trees, our spirit glides.
Every shadow, every light, a shared glance,
Woven silence invites us to dance.

Still Echoes in the Woodland Depths

In twilight's soft embrace, they sway,
The shadows dance in muted play.
Whispers weave through ancient trees,
Carried gently on the breeze.

A harmony of life abounds,
Resonating with nature's sounds.
Footfalls quiet on the ground,
In hollowed peace, stillness found.

Each rustling leaf, a tale untold,
Of secrets held in roots so bold.
The heartbeats echo, faint yet clear,
In solitude, we draw them near.

From mossy beds to starlit skies,
The woodland breathes, as time still flies.
Its silent grace, a soft goodnight,
In still echoes, we find our light.

Whispers of the Blooming Fern

Amidst the fronds, where shadows play,
The ferns arise to greet the day.
With emerald hues and graceful sway,
They whisper dreams in soft array.

In dappled light, their secrets share,
A rustling voice fills fragrant air.
Each leaf unfurls, a story spun,
In quiet moments, two become one.

The dew-kissed dawn brings whispers low,
Of hidden paths where few will go.
In every curve, in every line,
Life's fleeting dance begins to shine.

Their beauty speaks in gentle tones,
In woodland realms where time atones.
The blooming ferns, in silence, wait,
To share the peace that life creates.

The Invisible Thread of the Woodland Spirit

A thread unseen runs through the glade,
Binding each soul, a sacred braid.
Through vibrant leaves and tangled vines,
The spirit moves, in whispered signs.

It dances lightly on the winds,
A guide for lost, where hope begins.
With every step, it softly leads,
In harmony, our hearts it feeds.

From ancient oaks to streams that flow,
Its presence felt, yet never shown.
An echo faint, a pulse of life,
In harmony where all is rife.

The woodland spirit, ever near,
In silence sings its song sincere.
Through tangled roots and paths unknown,
We find our way, though not alone.

Beneath the Arching Boughs of Antiquity

Beneath the boughs that stretch so wide,
Where time and nature intertwine,
A world awakens, deep and true,
In shadows cast, our spirits renew.

Each age-old trunk, a sentinel stands,
Guarding stories of distant lands.
With branches steeped in tales of yore,
They beckon us to seek once more.

The dappled light, a painter's stroke,
Awakes the dreams that we invoke.
In rustling leaves, we hear the past,
A legacy that holds us fast.

Through seasons change and cycles blend,
New beginnings and the gentle end.
Beneath this dome of emerald grace,
We gather peace, we find our place.

Echoes from the Heart of Green

In the forest's gentle sway,
Leaves dance in sunlight's play,
Whispers of the ancient trees,
Carried softly on the breeze.

Moss blankets the rich brown earth,
Cradling secrets of their birth,
Ferns unfurl with tender grace,
Nature's touch, a warm embrace.

Birdsong weaves a melody,
Notes that breathe serenity,
Each flutter brings a sigh,
A symphony beneath the sky.

Beneath the arching boughs, we rest,
Finding peace, our hearts confessed,
In the stillness, love is found,
Echoes linger all around.

As twilight wraps the world in blue,
Stars awaken, bright and true,
Nature sleeps, but dreams take flight,
Echoes whisper through the night.

Dreaming in the Depths of the Thicket

In the thicket's embrace, I wander,
Lost in thoughts, sweet as a ponder,
Hidden pathways call my name,
In this realm, I'm never the same.

Shadows dance with flickering light,
Creatures stir in the hush of night,
Soft rustles pull me deeper still,
In the woods, I feel the thrill.

Dreams entwine with roots below,
Whispers of what the night may show,
Luminous fireflies softly gleam,
Painting pictures of a dream.

The air is rich with tales untold,
In every rustle, truth unfolds,
Time stands still, caught in the flow,
In this thicket, my spirit grows.

When dawn breaks the tender spell,
I carry fragments, heart will swell,
Dreams and echoes tightly knit,
In the thicket, forever lit.

Where Shadows Listen and Wait

In the corners where silence lies,
Shadows gather, wise and shy,
Hushed whispers speak of days gone by,
Holding secrets in their sigh.

Each crevice breathes a quiet tale,
A ghostly tune that will not pale,
From dusk until the break of dawn,
Where all the weary souls have gone.

Branches bend, and nighttime hums,
As darkness softens, the stillness drums,
Footsteps echo, stories blend,
In the shadow's arms, all wounds mend.

Flicker of lights, the stars align,
In this realm, the shadows shine,
Listening close, they cherish fate,
Where dreams are whispered, and shadows wait.

Fear not the dark, embrace the night,
For in its hold, there's hidden light,
Where shadows play their timeless game,
And listen softly, calling your name.

A Cathedral of Whispers

Within this grove, a sacred space,
Tall trees arch, their branches lace,
Murmurs float in tender air,
In this cathedral, hearts lay bare.

Sunbeams filter, a golden hue,
Softness settles on all that's true,
Each leaf a prayer, each breeze a song,
In this haven, we belong.

Echoes bounce from stone to stone,
Nature's voice, a gentle tone,
With every step on sacred ground,
A symphony of life is found.

The rustling leaves tell tales of old,
Whispers of love in stories told,
In this space where silence speaks,
In the heart of green, our spirit seeks.

As twilight falls, the stars ignite,
A tapestry of dreams takes flight,
In this cathedral, forever stand,
In whispered love, we join hand in hand.

Secrets Beneath the Boughs

Whispers weave through leaves so high,
Shadows dance where secrets lie.
Mossy carpets softly sigh,
Beneath the boughs, time slips by.

Hidden realms in twilight's glow,
Paths untrod, where breezes flow.
Echoes of a past we know,
Guarded dreams beneath the show.

Branches cradle stories old,
Nature's warmth, a heart of gold.
In the hush, the world unfolds,
Life's embrace, tender and bold.

Every rustle, every sigh,
Secrets shared as night draws nigh.
Beneath the boughs, we find our sky,
And in their shelter, hearts comply.

Nature's pulse, a rhythmic beat,
With whispers made of soft retreat.
Here beneath the boughs we meet,
In silence strong, our souls entreat.

Murmurs of the Hidden Grove

In a grove where shadows play,
Murmurs drift like light of day.
Each rustling leaf has tales to tell,
Secrets caught in nature's spell.

Underneath the canopy,
Voices blend in harmony.
Branches sway with ancient grace,
Echoing a timeless space.

Moonlit pathways gently glow,
Drawing forth the dreams we sow.
In the night, the stars align,
Murmurs sweet, the hearts entwine.

Crickets chirp their serenade,
As the night begins to fade.
In the grove, where whispers thrive,
We find the pulse of being alive.

Every sigh, each gentle breeze,
In the grove, the spirit frees.
Murmurs soft as twilight swells,
Stories of the forest, it tells.

Traces of the Moonlit Path

Crickets sing beneath the moon,
Footfalls echo, sweet and soon.
On the path of silver light,
Whispers cradle the velvet night.

Every step, a gentle grace,
Magic held in this embrace.
Moonlit traces guide the way,
Through the woods where shadows play.

Stars above, like lanterns glow,
Casting dreams on earth below.
Softly flows the midnight air,
In this silence, hearts lay bare.

Following where the shadows lead,
Each footfall plants a quiet seed.
Stories written in the night,
Traces of the pale moonlight.

Here beneath a sky of dreams,
Life unfolds in silvery beams.
On the path, our wishes blend,
As moonlit traces never end.

Where the Ferns Embrace

In the glen where ferns reside,
Nature's whispers softly glide.
Green embraces, lush and wide,
In their shade, the truths confide.

Rustling leaves, a sacred song,
Where the heart can feel belongs.
Ferns, like guardians, unite,
In their arms, we find our light.

Sunbeams filter through the green,
Crafting dreams that lie unseen.
In this haven, peace ignites,
Where the ferns cradle our nights.

Echoes of the earth's soft sigh,
Underneath the vast, blue sky.
In the embrace of nature's care,
All our worries float in air.

Sweet serenity we chase,
In the woods, where ferns embrace.
In their whispering, we find grace,
A timeless bond, a warm embrace.

Lullabies of the Woodland Shadows

In twilight's glow, soft whispers sway,
The branches hum a gentle play.
Stars blink down through leaves above,
Nature sings a song of love.

Crickets chirp, a timeworn tune,
Frogs croak softly, under the moon.
Night wraps all in velvet dark,
While fireflies dance, a fleeting spark.

The breeze weaves tales through tangled roots,
Owls hoot softly, in secret pursuits.
Each shadow holds a dreamer's heart,
A world of magic, where wonders start.

Moss blankets ground like a soft embrace,
In this serene and sacred space.
Whispers linger, in cool night air,
Woodland slumbers, without a care.

So close your eyes to the lullaby,
Let woodland's dreams gently pass by.
In every rustle, hear the call,
Of nature's peace, embracing all.

Echoing Silences in Green

Amidst the leaves, a silence reigns,
Soft shadows dance on winding lanes.
The world holds its breath, listening still,
To whispers of nature, ever so shrill.

Sunlight dapples through the trees,
A gentle warmth carried by the breeze.
Thoughts float softly, like petals in air,
In echoing silence, devoid of a care.

Each footstep muffled on carpet of moss,
Here time stands still, no need to cross.
In vibrant hues, the green unfolds,
Stories written in the earth, told.

Every rustle, a secret shared,
In hidden corners, where hearts are bared.
The symphony plays in quiet tones,
Even the stones have gentle moans.

In this cathedral of trees so grand,
Silences echo, hand in hand.
Close your eyes, let the stillness be,
In these green depths, forever free.

Beneath the Canopy's Embrace

Where sunlight kisses earth so sweet,
The woodland's heart finds its beat.
Leaves above weave patterns bright,
A tapestry of nature's light.

Beneath the canopy, time feels slow,
With every breath, the magic grows.
Speaking roots, with stories spun,
Dreams awakened, one by one.

The hidden paths call you near,
In whispered tones, they draw you here.
Mushrooms sprout in playful rings,
Nature's laughter lovingly sings.

Swaying branches sway and bend,
In this haven, hearts mend.
The melody of life intertwines,
A sacred bond where love defines.

In shadowed nooks, where secrets sleep,
The woodland's secrets, deep and deep.
Embrace the calm, let worries cease,
Here beneath the trees, find peace.

Shadows Dance in the Twilight

As day retreats and shadows bloom,
The dusk arrives, dispelling gloom.
Figures flit on gentle winds,
In twilight hours, the magic begins.

Cool air carries scents of pine,
Embraced by night, all feels divine.
Silhouettes sway with nature's breath,
In the fading light, we flirt with death.

Stars peek out, one by one,
Whispering tales of day now done.
Moonlight spills like silver paint,
On every leaf, soft and faint.

Through the woods, quiet shadows glide,
In every rustle, the world confides.
Echoes capture the night's sweet tease,
A dance of shadows through the trees.

Beneath the veil of dusk's embrace,
We lose ourselves in this sacred space.
In twilight's charm, our spirits soar,
As shadows dance forevermore.

Traces of the Moonlit Breeze

Whispers of night in the cool air,
Carried by winds that dance with care.
Stars shimmer softly, a distant glow,
Guiding lost souls where shadows flow.

Silver beams play on leaves so bright,
Painting the world in a dreamlike light.
Gentle sighs float on feathered wings,
Echoing tales that the silence brings.

A silken touch weaves through the trees,
Swaying with every fragrant breeze.
Memories linger in the soft sighs,
Kisses of night from the velvet skies.

Pathways of silver and muted grey,
Lead the heart where the wild things play.
In the stillness, a soft heartbeat thumps,
Nature's rhythm, a dance that jumps.

Each moment captured, a fleeting glance,
Held in the magic of night's sweet trance.
The moon hangs low, a guardian bright,
Watching over dreams that take flight.

Lost in the Underbrush

In tangled thickets where shadows creep,
Secrets lie buried, hidden deep.
The scent of moss and damp earth rise,
A world alive beneath the skies.

Branches intertwine in a twisted maze,
Whispers echo from the distant days.
Footsteps muffled on soft, damp ground,
In this wild realm, peace can be found.

A rustling sound, the heartbeat of life,
Songs of the forest, free from strife.
Sunlight filters through leaves above,
Nature's embrace, an endless love.

With every turn, a new surprise,
Creatures hidden with curious eyes.
The underbrush holds tales untold,
In the quiet, mysteries unfold.

Lost in a world where time stands still,
Every moment offers a gentle thrill.
In nature's arms, I find my way,
Guided by whispers of the day.

Dreaming in the Dappled Light

Sunbeams filter through branches high,
Creating patterns like a painter's sigh.
On the forest floor, shadows play,
Leading the heart where dreams gently sway.

Mushrooms flourish in emerald beds,
A quilt of life where nature treads.
Every flutter speaks to the soul,
In this green haven, the senses stroll.

Butterflies dance on the whispered breeze,
Twisting and turning with effortless ease.
Colors burst forth like a painter's delight,
In the embrace of the dappled light.

Songs of birds weave through the air,
Harmony lingers, a soothing prayer.
In this moment, all worries cease,
Nature cradles the heart in peace.

Dreams intertwine in a tapestry bright,
Woven by magic, kissed by light.
Here in the woods, joy takes flight,
Suspended in time, beneath the height.

A Reverie of Rustling Leaves

In the gentle hush of an autumn eve,
Leaves murmur tales, entice and weave.
Gold and amber flutter with grace,
Whispering secrets in a soft embrace.

Each rustle carries a hint of cheer,
Nature's lullaby for the soul to hear.
Under the canopy, shadows shift,
Bringing the heart a wondrous gift.

The wind plays softly, a restless song,
Inviting dreams as we wander along.
Every crackle, a promise made,
In the moment's peace, worries fade.

Memories dance with each falling leaf,
A bittersweet touch, a joyful grief.
In the golden glow of a twilight's haze,
Life's simple joys ignite in a blaze.

A reverie sparked by the evening's kiss,
In nature's arms, a tranquil bliss.
Lost in the magic of rustling sounds,
Our hearts united where love abounds.

Lost in the Hush of the Foliage

In the whisper of green, I stand tall,
Lost to the buzzing, a soft, gentle call.
Shadows dance lightly on the forest floor,
Nature's own lullaby, forevermore.

Waves of silence wash over my soul,
As the branches weave, they create a whole.
Colors shimmer bright under the sun's gaze,
Wrapped in this moment, I linger and gaze.

Time feels suspended in the dense embrace,
Each breath a blessing in this sacred space.
Here, I am free, in a world of my own,
Lost in the hush where wild dreams are sown.

A breeze carries secrets that no one can hear,
Tender memories echo, ever so clear.
The rustle of leaves, a soft, sweet refrain,
Cocooned in this hush, I have all to gain.

So let me disappear into this green nest,
Where silence and solace give way to rest.
A journey within, as the foliage sighs,
In whispers of peace, the heart ever flies.

Lurking Presence of Quiet Beasts

In shadows they sit, with eyes sharp and bright,
Quietly watching, in the cloak of the night.
Low growls and whispers, they prowl and they creep,
Guardians of secrets, in silence they sleep.

Every rustle tells tales of their grace,
Silent hunters hiding, they own this place.
With fur like the dusk, they blend with the gray,
And under the moonlight, they silently sway.

Yet in the stillness, there's beauty to find,
Within the presence of creatures confined.
They teach us the art of the moment, the pause,
In the lurking of beasts, we discover a cause.

To honor the whispers of nature's lost kin,
The guardians of twilight, so wild and so thin.
In the woodlands and thickets, their essence remains,
As we wander wide-eyed, breaking free from our chains.

So listen closely, the wild holds its breath,
In the lurking of beasts, feel the dance with death.
It's a tale of survival, both fierce and yet meek,
In the heart of the quiet, they whisper and speak.

Meditative Unraveling of the Canopy

Above, the branches weave tales of old,
In a tapestry lush, their stories unfold.
A soft rustle echoes, a gentle embrace,
As light dapples down, it creates a space.

In this sanctuary where shadows reside,
The canopy dances, with secrets to hide.
Each leaf drips with wisdom, age etched in time,
In the heart of the forest, nature's pure rhyme.

With every deep breath, I feel them unspool,
The threads of existence, the silence, the rule.
Boundaries break as I wander below,
In the meditative calm, the world starts to glow.

Nature's own whispers, like notes on a page,
Crossing the threshold, breaking free from the cage.
Patterns of life weave and swirl all around,
In the rustle of leaves, true presence is found.

Amidst this great canopy, I let my heart soar,
In the unraveling moment, I seek to explore.
A place free of judgment, of chatter, of noise,
In the soft, silent depths, I find my true voice.

Haven of the Slumbering Leaves

Upon the forest floor, a carpet of dreams,
Where all of life's whispers merge into streams.
Each leaf a soft pillow, a refuge so sweet,
A haven for weary, where heartbeats retreat.

Echoes of nature, laid bare in the ground,
In the hush of the glade, peace quietly found.
Amongst ancient boughs, my spirit can rest,
In the cradle of leaves, truly blessed.

Soft lullabies sung by the rustling trees,
Carry me gently on a shimmering breeze.
A kingdom of calm, where the heart learns to heal,
In the depth of the silence, life's wonders reveal.

So here I will linger, amidst tranquil sighs,
Where dreams weave through branches that touch the
skies.
With nature as guardian, I shed all my fears,
In the haven of leaves, I am washed clean of tears.

I am free as a bird, in this sacred retreat,
With each breath of the forest, my soul will complete.
A bond with the earth, in the soft, gentle light,
In the haven of slumbering leaves, all feels right.

Whispers of Starlit Nights

Beneath the velvet sky so bright,
Whispers carried on the breeze,
Dancing shadows in the light,
Nighttime's gentle mysteries.

Stars above like diamonds shine,
Telling tales of ages past,
In this moment, all feels fine,
Echoes of the night hold fast.

Moonbeams touch the sleeping ground,
Softly hugging weary dreams,
In the quiet, magic found,
Life unfolds in silver streams.

Stars will fade with dawn's embrace,
Yet they'll linger in our hearts,
Carrying the night's sweet grace,
A reminder when day starts.

Whispers linger in my soul,
Guiding me through every plight,
In the dark, I find my role,
Listening close to starlit night.

The Quiet Pulse of Forest Life

In the woods where silence reigns,
A heartbeat echoes through the trees,
Life pulsates in gentle strains,
Whispers of the softest breeze.

Mossy carpets cradle feet,
Ferns unfurl in emerald light,
Nature's rhythm, calm and sweet,
In the shadows, takes its flight.

Birds awaken with the dawn,
Singing praises, clear and bright,
Each note woven, dusk to dawn,
A symphony of pure delight.

From the brook, a soothing sound,
Ripples dance upon the stone,
In this haven, peace is found,
In the forest, I am home.

Time stands still with every breath,
Whispers echo from the past,
In the wild, defying death,
True serenity at last.

Beneath the Maple's Watchful Gaze

Under branches, broad and wise,
Maple leaves in shades of gold,
Whispers drift, a soft reprise,
Stories of the young and old.

In the shade, the world feels slow,
Time suspended, moments sigh,
Gentle winds begin to blow,
Beneath the vast and open sky.

Roots embrace the earth below,
Holding secrets, ancient lore,
Every whisper, like a flow,
Bonding nature evermore.

As the light begins to fade,
Colors burst, a vibrant show,
Maple's beauty never staid,
In the twilight's gentle glow.

Underneath its watchful gaze,
We find solace, peace, and grace,
In the heart of autumn's phase,
Nature holds a warm embrace.

An Ode to Quietude

In a world of endless noise,
Quietude, a precious gift,
Speaking softly, calm restores,
In the stillness, spirits lift.

Moments pause, the heart takes flight,
Embracing calm, we breathe in deep,
In the shadows of the night,
Solitude, a promise to keep.

Waves of silence wash the shore,
Cleansing worries, doubts, and fears,
In this place, we are yet more,
Finding solace, shedding tears.

Each heartbeat whispers through the dark,
Painting memories with each sigh,
In the quiet, we embark,
On a journey, we map the sky.

With each breath, an ode we sing,
To the peace that silence yields,
In the quiet, joy takes wing,
Nature's song in hearts revealed.

Secrets Wrapped in Verdant Layers

In shadows deep where whispers soar,
Among the ferns, the shadows explore.
Life hides beneath the emerald guise,
Unlocking truths through nature's eyes.

A tapestry of green and gold,
Guarding stories that remain untold.
Underneath the ancient trees,
The forest breathes, it calls with ease.

Each rustling leaf, a sigh or tune,
Beneath the watchful eye of moon.
Nature's secrets, softly spun,
In tangled roots, the stories run.

A heart of earth, a soul so free,
In every shadow, mystery.
Nestled deep in tranquil glades,
Life dances softly, joy pervades.

With every step, in silence creep,
Through verdant layers, secrets keep.
Nature's hand, a gentle guide,
In this embrace, the truths abide.

Treading Softly on the Veiled Path

With each step, the silence hums,
As morning breaks and softly drums.
Veiled in mist, the journey flows,
In hidden realms where magic grows.

Treading softly where shadows play,
On this path, I weave and sway.
Whispers gather in the air,
A timeless dance, a breath laid bare.

The trees align like ancient guards,
Each crown a kingdom, dreams as shards.
Nature beckons, old and wise,
In every crevice, truth arises.

The winding road, a tender friend,
With secrets that it will not send.
Footsteps soft, a gentle touch,
In the stillness, I find so much.

Beneath the layers of leaf and bud,
Life murmurs in the shifting mud.
A veiled path where echoes sing,
In this journey, peace I bring.

Solitude Beneath the Twisted Trunks

Beneath the twisted, aged limbs,
Where sunlight fades and shadow dims.
In solitude, the heart finds peace,
As Nature's sighs help worries cease.

Entwined in roots, a world so vast,
Time slips by, the moments last.
Here I linger, thoughts like streams,
Flowing gently into dreams.

Among the trunks, whispers ignite,
Holding secrets wrapped in night.
Every crack and every curl,
In silent wonder, I unfurl.

The symphony of rustling bark,
In solitude, I find my spark.
Nature's voice, a gentle call,
In this embrace, I rise, I fall.

Twisted trunks tell tales of yore,
As I listen, I crave for more.
Here beneath the ancient trees,
My spirit dances in the breeze.

Harmonies of the Rustling Leaf

In twilight hours, the leaves take flight,
Swaying softly in the fading light.
Each whisper tells of tales once spun,
A harmony where all is one.

The melody of rustling trees,
Carries secrets upon the breeze.
In every flutter, echoes rise,
A song composed beneath the skies.

The forest hums a sacred tune,
With each wave, a dance in June.
Leaves entwined in nature's sway,
In this symphony, I long to stay.

With every breath, the world unfolds,
In timeless rhythms, stories told.
Harmony cradles night and day,
A tranquil heart at ease, I lay.

Rustling leaves like gentle hands,
Weaving comfort through the lands.
In nature's choir, I hear the call,
A melody that unites us all.

The Stillness of Old Growth

In the shade where whispers hide,
The ancient trees stand side by side.
Moss blankets roots in green embrace,
Time stands still in this sacred space.

Sunbeams dance on leaves above,
Nature's silence, a gentle shove.
Each breath carries a tale untold,
Of wisdom held in barks so bold.

Rustling leaves tell secrets deep,
Where shadows move and memories sleep.
A symphony of nature's call,
In this realm, we feel so small.

Branches arch like open arms,
Protecting life from worldly harms.
In stillness, beauty reigns supreme,
A tranquil, ever-living dream.

Beneath the sky, so vast, so wide,
The old growth stands, a timeless guide.
In quietude, our spirits soar,
In the stillness, we seek for more.

Veiled in Verdant Dreams

A curtain of green, a soft embrace,
Whispers of magic fill this space.
Leaves glisten like jewels in the light,
Nature's tapestry, pure and bright.

In shadows where the ferns do sway,
Every step is like a ballet.
Life unfolds in layers of grace,
In this world, we find our place.

Murmurs of streams in hidden trails,
Echoing through the wind's soft gales.
Fleeting glimpses of creatures rare,
In verdant dreams, they linger, share.

Through tangled vines, the heart takes flight,
Awash in colors, a pure delight.
This waking dream, an endless flow,
Where verdant wonders constantly grow.

The air is thick with fragrant blooms,
In every corner, life resumes.
Veiled in dreams, we dare to roam,
In love with nature, we find home.

Serene Steps Over Soft Earth

Underfoot, the earth is kind,
Whispers of nature intertwined.
Each step forward, a gentle sigh,
In harmony, we drift and fly.

The path is woven with past and present,
Alive with stories, vibrant, pleasant.
Sunlight dapples through the trees,
Serenity rides on the breeze.

Petals fall like whispered prayers,
Scattered blessings, nature cares.
In quiet moments, we find peace,
In each heartbeat, worries cease.

Soft earth embraces weary feet,
With every footprint, life's heartbeat.
Nature's pulse beneath the sky,
Reminds us all to breathe and try.

As twilight whispers a sweet refrain,
We wander softly, free from pain.
Serene steps lead us to the heart,
Where all our journeys find their start.

The Forgotten Path

A narrow trail, overgrown and lost,
Each step forward, we bear the cost.
Time has draped a shroud of green,
Yet whispers call from places unseen.

Cracked stones lead to silent glades,
Where echoes of laughter slowly fade.
In the shadows, history breathes,
In every branch, a story weaves.

The air is thick with tales untold,
Of dreams forgotten, hearts grown bold.
Nature reclaims what once was there,
A gentle hug, a soft repair.

Beneath the boughs, the path entwines,
With hidden treasures, tangled signs.
Lost in wonder, we roam with ease,
On this forgotten trail through the trees.

Each twist and turn, a step in time,
A pathway rich with nature's rhyme.
As daylight fades, we find our way,
The forgotten path calls us to stay.

Among the Giants of Time

In shadows deep, the giants stand,
Their roots entwined with ancient land.
Whispers of ages brush the ground,
A testament to life profound.

Beneath their boughs, the secrets dwell,
In every ring, a tale to tell.
Time's gentle hands, they wear with grace,
Each season finds its rightful place.

The sunlit paths, the moonlit nights,
Guardian trees under starlit heights.
Amidst their might, we feel so small,
Yet in their shade, we find our all.

Leaves rustle softly, stories glide,
In silence, history does not hide.
Among the giants, we take our stand,
In reverence for the nurturing hand.

So let us tread with mindful care,
For in their presence, love we share.
Among the giants, forever we roam,
Finding in their roots, our eternal home.

Nature's Lament in Twilit Silence

In twilight's grasp, the echoes sigh,
As nature mourns a fading sky.
With every breeze, a whisper low,
A soft lament for life's sweet flow.

The crickets sing their evening tune,
Beneath the watchful gaze of the moon.
Stars blink softly, tears in the night,
For what was lost in fading light.

The river flows with heavy heart,
Carrying wishes, dreams to part.
In silence deep, the shadows blend,
As day concedes, the night to send.

The rustling leaves, they seem to weep,
In nature's arms, the secrets keep.
The cycle turns; the world must grieve,
In twilit silence, we believe.

Yet with each dawn, the hope will rise,
In every heart, a new surprise.
Through nature's tears, life will persist,
In this lament, we still exist.

The Curl of a Leaf's Whisper

Upon the breeze, a leaf takes flight,
A gentle twist in morning light.
Its curl holds secrets of the past,
Whispers of seasons, fading fast.

Once vibrant green, now amber hue,
It dances gracefully, ever new.
Carried by winds to places unknown,
A soft farewell in nature's tone.

In gardens still, its story's spun,
Of sunlit days and evening sun.
Each rustling sound, a tale retold,
In every crevice, the world unfolds.

From branch to ground, the journey flows,
The cycle of life endlessly shows.
Nature's breath in every swirl,
The silent heart of a leaf's twirl.

So pause and listen, hear the plea,
Of life's brief moments, wild and free.
The curl of a leaf, a voice in the air,
A whisper of beauty that lingers rare.

Unheard Echoes from Ageless Trees

In the stillness, where shadows play,
The ageless trees hold time at bay.
Their branches sway with wise intent,
In every creak, a message sent.

From root to crown, their spirits flow,
Through seasons harsh, yet still they grow.
In bark and leaf, the echoes hum,
Whispers of ages, soft and numb.

The tales of storms that made them bend,
The gentle rains that love extend.
In every knot, the past resides,
Unheard echoes where history hides.

The forest breathes with ancient grace,
In their embrace, we find our place.
Listening close, we hear their calls,
The timeless wisdom that never falls.

So next time you wander through the glade,
Take heed of the whispers the trees have made.
Unheard echoes from ageless trees,
A symphony played on a gentle breeze.

The Breath of Ancient Roots

In the shadow of old trees,
Whispers dance in the breeze,
Stories cradle the ground,
Time's embrace all around.

Branches stretch to the skies,
In silence, wisdom lies,
Roots twist in ancient soil,
Life's essence, rich and royal.

Every leaf tells a tale,
Of love, loss, and the frail,
A tapestry of years,
Woven with laughter and tears.

Beneath the stars so bright,
Echoes shimmer in the night,
The past and present meet,
In rhythms soft and sweet.

With every breath we take,
New paths and journeys make,
Embracing what has been,
In every heartbeat, kin.

Rustling Silence

Quiet thoughts drift like leaves,
Between whispers the heart grieves,
Stillness wraps the night tight,
Shadows fade with the light.

Crisp air holds secrets dear,
In the hush, whispers appear,
Echoes of dreams long lost,
The soul counts every cost.

In the dark, a spark glows,
Flickering where no one knows,
A pulse beneath the calm,
Woven with nature's balm.

Through the rustling of the trees,
Soft murmurs float with ease,
Embracing the quietude,
In stillness, find a mood.

Here, where moments collide,
In silence, let thoughts slide,
Rest in the arms of night,
Until day breaks with light.

A Lullaby for the Lost

Close your weary eyes,
Underneath the starry skies,
Dreams of hope softly weave,
In twilight, take your leave.

For the ones gone astray,
In shadows they softly play,
Whispers call through the mist,
In memory, they persist.

Let the moonlight guide home,
Each heart that seems to roam,
With a song sweet and low,
In the night, let love glow.

Rest your head, dear soul,
In the darkness, be whole,
For in dreams, they sing,
Of the love that they bring.

A lullaby that transcends,
Hearts unite, mending bends,
In this peaceful embrace,
Find solace, find your place.

Where Light Meets Shade

At the edge of dawn's light,
Silhouettes dance, taking flight,
Colors blend in gentle streams,
Awakening day from dreams.

The sun spills gold on leaves,
In the shade, the heart believes,
Nature hums its serene tune,
Beneath the watchful moon.

Where shadows stretch and play,
Life breathes in a soft sway,
In the clamor of the day,
Whispers of peace find their way.

Each moment, a quiet grace,
Where light and dark interlace,
In the balance, find the truth,
Awash in the flow of youth.

As dusk brings the night near,
In stillness, drop every fear,
For in the twilight's embrace,
Light and shade share a space.

Veils of Mist Amongst the Bark

Veils of mist drape the trees,
Whispering secrets in the breeze.
Branches arch like ancient bones,
Nature sings in softest tones.

Shadows dance in tender light,
Lost in dreams, we take our flight.
Fingers trace the sculpted rind,
Magic woven, undefined.

Every sigh, a gentle breath,
Woodland echoes life and death.
Hushed desires take their shape,
In every bend, a haunting cape.

Footsteps fade on mossy ground,
In the silence, we are found.
Crickets play their evening tune,
While fireflies rise like a boon.

Veils of mist, our dreams in flight,
Lost in heartbeats of the night.
Wrapped in wonder, we abide,
In the woods, our spirits glide.

The Quiet Reverie of Twilight Glades

In twilight glades where shadows blend,
The day whispers its gentle end.
Softly hues of blue and gold,
Stitch the fabric of the bold.

Crickets stir as night awakes,
With every breath, our caution breaks.
Moonbeams spill like silken thread,
Curtains drawn, our worries shed.

Here the stars begin to shine,
In the hush, our hearts align.
Every sparkle maps the path,
Of dreams, we find within their wrath.

The quiet night, a tender muse,
In stillness, we shall not refuse.
Nature's call is soft and clear,
In these glades, the world we steer.

With every sigh, the heart expands,
Lost in time, with open hands.
We'll wander where the wild things play,
In twilight's arms, we drift away.

Silence Speaks Amongst the Roots

Amongst the roots, where whispers dwell,
Silence weaves a secret spell.
Echos of the earth below,
In every sigh, the ancients flow.

Fingers brush the knotted ground,
Where memories of old abound.
Each twisted vine and tempered bark,
Holds the tales when time was stark.

Starlit nights, a canvas wide,
In this silence, we confide.
The pulse of life, a steady thrum,
In nature's cave, we become.

With roots entwined, we seek to find,
The stories left by humankind.
In every shadow, truth reveals,
What silence speaks, the heart feels.

Beneath the soil, the world spins slow,
In quietude, we learn to grow.
Amidst the roots where shadows dance,
Life's eternal, in our trance.

Timeless Embrace of the Leafy Realm

In the leafy realm, a whisper calls,
Beneath the canopy where shadows fall.
Embraced by nature, we find our space,
Time dissolves in this sacred place.

Gentle breezes stroke our skin,
In every rustle, life begins.
Branches weave a tapestry,
Of moments lost in reverie.

Sunlight drips like golden dew,
Each ray a promise, fresh and new.
Wildflowers bloom with grace untold,
In vibrant hues, the stories unfold.

Roots entwine, a sacred bond,
In every heartbeat, we respond.
To nature's rhythm, slow and deep,
In leafy realms, our souls will leap.

Timeless embrace in verdant halls,
Where laughter dances, and silence calls.
A sanctuary of gentle dreams,
In leafy whispers, our spirit gleams.

Muffled Footfalls on Soft Moss

In the quiet woods we roam,
Footfalls softened by the green,
Whispers dance upon the breeze,
Nature sings where leaves convene.

Sunlight trickles through the trees,
Casting shadows, warm and light,
Each step taken, calm and slow,
In this haven, hearts take flight.

Mossy carpets, deep and plush,
Cushion every gentle tread,
Here, the world fades to a hush,
Leaving naught but thought unsaid.

A squirrel darts with fleeting grace,
While ferns sway, a quiet sigh,
Life unfolds at nature's pace,
Underneath the reaching sky.

In this realm of peace and calm,
Every breath feels fresh and new,
Muffled footfalls, soft as balm,
Connecting us to what is true.

The Unseen Conversations

In shadows linger whispers low,
Echoes of a thought long passed,
Unseen words in silence flow,
Moments captured, meant to last.

The breeze carries tales untold,
Secrets flutter as they play,
Leaves confide in tones of gold,
Beneath the sun's warm, watchful ray.

Voices drift on corners bright,
Each glance holds a story deep,
Silent musings take to flight,
In the night, they softly creep.

Stars converse in twinkling lights,
A dance upon the velvet sea,
Bringing dreams to eager sights,
Opening paths for what could be.

In the stillness of the hour,
Conversations weave and bend,
Unseen threads, an unseen power,
Binding all that we hold dear.

Secrets Among the Branches

Hidden truths in leaves entwined,
Stories kept from prying eyes,
Nature's cloak is well-defined,
Guarding whispers of the skies.

Branches sway with gentle ease,
Carrying their weight of time,
Every rustle holds a tease,
A rhythm, nature's whispered rhyme.

Between the boughs, tales take flight,
Of lovers, dreams, and distant lands,
Buffered underneath the night,
Each secret told with gentle hands.

Ready hearts, the forest speaks,
With every rustling gentle breeze,
The quiet hush, it softly seeks,
To unveil all the mysteries.

From acorns to the mighty oak,
Life's essence flows through roots below,
In the branch's sway, secrets spoke,
An ancient truth, a sacred glow.

Gossamer Threads of Thought

Delicate as dawn's first light,
Thoughts emerge like misty dreams,
Floating softly, feather-light,
Woven in the sun's warm beams.

Each whisper spins a fragile thread,
Intertwining with the air,
In this web of hopes well-fed,
Ideas dance without a care.

Waves of inspiration rise,
Shimmering in the quiet space,
Crafted by the mind's disguise,
Unfolding with the gentlest grace.

In the heart of silence, gleam
Fragments of what could be real,
Gossamer threads weave a dream,
In the stillness, thoughts conceal.

Through the lattice of the soul,
Every notion finds its way,
Lighting paths to make us whole,
Guiding spirits in the sway.

The Guardian of the Glade

In shadows deep, where whispers dwell,
The guardian stands, a silent shell.
With ancient roots and gentle grace,
He watches over this sacred space.

Through rustling leaves, the stories flow,
Of creatures small and trees that grow.
His heart entwined with nature's song,
A bond unbroken, steady and strong.

The dew-kissed dawn, a soft embrace,
Reflects the light upon his face.
He whispers secrets to the air,
And guides the lost with tender care.

As twilight falls and stars appear,
His presence calms our deepest fear.
With every breath, the glade alive,
In harmony, all spirits strive.

The guardian knows, though time may fade,
The love for life will never trade.
In peace, he stands, forever bold,
A timeless tale within the fold.

In the Heart of Stillness

In the heart of stillness, shadows blend,
Where quiet thoughts and feelings mend.
The softest breeze through branches sways,
A timeless moment, lost in days.

Rippling waters whisper low,
Secrets of the earth below.
Petals kiss the morning dew,
Nature's canvas, fresh and new.

Beneath the boughs, in quiet grace,
Life finds its rhythm, finds its place.
A symphony of rustling leaves,
In this still realm, the spirit weaves.

The sun dips low, a golden hue,
Painting dreams in shades of blue.
Here we breathe, our worries cease,
In the heart of stillness, we find peace.

Moments linger, pure and bright,
In nature's hold, we feel the light.
A gentle sigh, the world stands still,
In sacred solace, hearts can fill.

Refrains of Nature's Secrets

In rustling leaves, a secret shared,
Refrains of nature, deep and rare.
The song of streams, the call of night,
In every pause, a spark of light.

From mountain high to valley low,
A melody in whispers flow.
The echo of the eagle's flight,
Cascades of joy that feel so right.

The flicker of the fireflies dance,
Inviting us to take a chance.
To heed the call of ancient trees,
A harmony upon the breeze.

In twilight's glow, the world awakes,
A symphony that never breaks.
With every breath, our spirits rise,
Refrains of nature, timeless ties.

So listen close, the world will sing,
Of life and love, and all that spring.
In the heart of silence, truth reflects,
The beauty found in nature's depths.

A Gentle Heartbeat in the Wild

In the wild where wonders bloom,
A gentle heartbeat stirs the room.
With every pulse, the creatures thrive,
In sync with nature, they come alive.

The rustle of the grass below,
A heartbeat tuned to nature's flow.
The fluttering wings in morning light,
Awake the world, dispel the night.

From streams that babble to the trees,
Each breath we take, a moment frees.
In quiet woods, the spirits dance,
In every glance, there's pure romance.

The whisper of the gentle breeze,
Holds tales of life among the trees.
A bond unbroken, silent yet loud,
A gentle heartbeat, nature proud.

As sunsets paint the sky above,
We find in nature's heart, pure love.
For in the wild, we truly feel,
The gentle heartbeat, strong and real.

Tranquil Requiem Amongst the Pines

Whispers dance on the breeze,
Tall pines stand in calm repose.
Nature sings its softest tunes,
Underneath the moonlight's glow.

Shadows stretch as daylight fades,
Stars awaken in the night.
Branches sway with gentle grace,
Cradling dreams in silver light.

Echoes of the forest speak,
Through the rustling of the leaves.
Each note a sacred secret,
Carried on the evening's eaves.

Footsteps trace a path to peace,
Heartbeats sync with nature's song.
In this tranquil, timeless space,
Where all our worries feel so wrong.

As the night wraps all in hush,
Moments linger, softly glide.
In this requiem among pines,
Our souls are free, as hearts abide.

Sylvan Soliloquy

In the woods where silence reigns,
Softly spoken words are heard.
Trees converse with ancient tales,
Every rustle, every bird.

Mossy carpets underfoot,
With each step, a world unfolds.
Sunbeams filter through the leaves,
Painting stories yet untold.

From the brook a melody,
Whispers carried with the stream.
Nature hums a gentle tune,
Invoking every fleeting dream.

Breezes tease the branches' tips,
Nature's brush paints skies of blue.
In this sylvan solitude,
All our cares become anew.

Within these woods, our spirits soar,
Finding peace in every sound.
Lost in thought, yet found in grace,
In this haven, love is found.

Nature's Hidden Heartbeat

In the glade where shadows dwell,
Pulse of life beneath the skin.
Every rustle, every sigh,
Nature's heartbeat, deep within.

Moss and ferns in damp embrace,
Whisper secrets, soft and low.
Roots entwine and intertwine,
Tales of ages come and go.

Leaves partake in sun's sweet grace,
Dancing softly in the breeze.
Every flutter, every rustle,
Marks the rhythm of the trees.

Burbling brooks and buzzing bees,
Echoes of vitality.
Hidden hearts beat louder here,
In this forest, wild and free.

Take a moment, breathe it in,
Feel the pulse of earth around.
In nature's arms, we find our place,
Here, our hearts are unbound.

Stillness Wrapped in Leaves

Golden hues of autumn's breath,
Crunching softly underfoot.
Quiet wraps the world in peace,
Nature sings in undertones soot.

Branches bow with weary grace,
Bearing the weight of fading light.
Stillness reigns within the woods,
As day surrenders into night.

Crimson leaves like whispered dreams,
Float to earth in gentle swirls.
Time slows down within this space,
As twilight begins to unfurl.

Moonlight spills on gentle streams,
Reflections dance on midnight's themes.
In the hush of evening's cloak,
Life takes pause, or so it seems.

Gather close, let worries cease,
In this calm, we find our ease.
Wrapped in stillness, draped in peace,
Amongst the leaves, our souls release.

Breath of the Still Morningforest

Whispers of dawn in the glade,
The sun peeks through branches laid.
Gentle mist hugs the ground tight,
Awakening life in soft light.

Birds trill sweet songs from above,
Nature hums, a melody of love.
Leaves dance lightly in the breeze,
A tranquil moment, hearts at ease.

Footsteps tread on a quiet path,
Finding solace in nature's math.
Ferns unfurl as shadows creep,
In this beauty, the world sleeps.

Rays of gold paint the forest floor,
Each breath is a gift, forever more.
Scent of pine fills the crisp air,
In morning's arms, we find repair.

Time slows down in this embrace,
Nature's pulse at its own pace.
The wild speaks in gentle tones,
In stillness, we find our home.

The Storehouse of Memories in Green

Amidst the trees, stories grow,
In shadows deep, soft winds blow.
Whispers echo from the past,
A treasure trove, vast and vast.

Leaves canvas dreams in every hue,
Each flutter tells of journeys true.
Time weaves tales in bark and stone,
Cradle of secrets, we feel at home.

Sunlight dapples through the trees,
Each ray sparks cherished memories.
Roots entwine, the ground holds tight,
Embracing all in gentle light.

Laughter lingers in the air,
Moments shared beyond compare.
Nature's heart beats strong and loud,
Cocooned within its verdant shroud.

Hope blooms bright in every glen,
A sanctuary for all beings, kin.
In stillness woven like a seam,
This green storehouse holds every dream.

Voices Written in the Bark

Carved in time, the stories speak,
In gnarled lines, we find the weak.
Each knot a whisper, path revealed,
Nature's library, gently sealed.

Fingers trace where words once flowed,
Life's ink on wood, a heavy load.
The silent witnesses of our days,
In their embrace, our hearts ablaze.

Leaves murmur secrets to the winds,
Echoes of laughter, where it begins.
The forest holds what we forget,
A tapestry of joy and regret.

Seasons change, yet tales remain,
Anaheim whispers, soft like rain.
Moss-clad tomes of ancient lore,
In every ring, the spirit soars.

In the bark, the past collides,
With every glance, a heart abides.
Voices rise as the shadows dance,
In sacred woods, we take our chance.

Night's Tranquility Amidst the Grove

Beneath the stars, the forest sighs,
A peaceful hush cloaks the skies.
Moonbeams trickle through the leaves,
In this night, the spirit believes.

Crickets serenade the dark,
A symphony, nature's spark.
Whispers float on a soft breeze,
As shadows weave through the trees.

In twilight's arms, dreams take flight,
Each heartbeat echoes through the night.
The grove holds tales both old and new,
In silent corners, secrets brew.

Stars twinkle like forgotten dreams,
Illuminating night's gentle schemes.
In moonlit pools, reflections dance,
Inviting dreams with every glance.

Time stills as the world moves on,
In this magic, hope is drawn.
Night's embrace, a soothing balm,
Amidst the grove, we find our calm.

Nature's Quiet Confession

Whispers in the rustling leaves,
Soft secrets on the breeze.
Echoes of the brook's pure flow,
Nature's tales begin to grow.

Sunlight filters through the trees,
Dancing shadows with such ease.
Flowers bloom, a vibrant hue,
Each a story, old yet new.

Mountains stand with ancient grace,
Guarding time in their embrace.
Birds take flight in morning's light,
Singing songs of pure delight.

Clouds drift lazily up high,
Painting murals in the sky.
Every color speaks so loud,
Nature's canvas, rich and proud.

As the day begins to wane,
Evening whispers call again.
In this calm, the heart finds rest,
Nature's peace is truly blessed.

Hushed Trails of Time

Footsteps softly press the ground,
In the silence, secrets found.
Where the wildflowers intertwine,
Time stands still along the line.

Ancient boughs reach up to sky,
Fingers tracing where the days lie.
Each stone holds a tale, a name,
Whispers of a lost acclaim.

With each breeze, a memory sighs,
Beneath the vast and watchful skies.
Nature's clock ticks soft and slow,
In this haven, time will flow.

Shadows stretch as daylight fades,
In the twilight, magic wades.
Each moment wrapped in gentle glow,
Hushed trails where the spirits go.

With the night, the stars ignite,
Guiding lost souls in their flight.
Through these trails, forever bound,
In whispers, love and peace are found.

Beneath the Veil of Green

Underneath the leafy shroud,
Life awakens, pure and loud.
Roots entwined in earthy grace,
Hidden worlds in this embrace.

Sunlit spots where shadows play,
Brighten up the verdant way.
Insects hum a gentle tune,
Nature's symphony in bloom.

Mossy carpets cradle feet,
Nature's cradle, soft and sweet.
Here the heart can find its peace,
Beneath the green, all worries cease.

Ferns unfurl with every breath,
Life persists in subtle death.
Every petal, every vine,
Tells a story, intricate design.

In the stillness, secrets wake,
In this haven, hearts can break.
Yet beneath that veil so green,
Life persists, forever seen.

Twilight's Silent Watch

As the sun dips low and shy,
Night's embrace begins to sigh.
Stars awaken, soft and bright,
Guardians in the tranquil night.

Moonlit paths of silver grace,
Echoes linger in this space.
Every shadow, deep and tall,
Whispers secrets, nature's call.

Crickets sing a lullaby,
While the owls in silence fly.
In this hour, dreams take flight,
Cradled in the arms of night.

Gentle winds through branches weave,
Soft caresses, hearts believe.
Here beneath the twilight's watch,
Time stands still, its hands beseech.

Under stars, our hopes collide,
In the dark, we're not denied.
Twilight holds our deepest fears,
Wrapped in silence, kissed by tears.

The Forgotten Echo

In the quiet woods, a whisper trails,
Footsteps lost in forgotten tales.
Shadows dance where memories play,
Fading slowly, day by day.

Echoes linger in the air,
Haunting tunes call everywhere.
Voices of those who've come and gone,
In the silence, they live on.

Time stands still in this sacred space,
Nature's charm, a warm embrace.
Rustling leaves, a soft sigh,
Carrying stories, never to die.

Beneath the branches, secrets lie,
Silent witnesses to the sky.
In this realm where shadows merge,
The echoes of the past emerge.

Listen close, let your heart feel,
The forgotten echoes, raw and real.
In the solitude, find your peace,
Embrace the stillness, let it cease.

Enchanted Shadows of the Glen

Where sunlight flecks the forest floor,
Enchanted shadows weave and soar.
Whispers tell of ancient dreams,
Nestled soft in nature's seams.

Moss-covered stones, a hidden trail,
Fairy lights in the evening pale.
Rippling streams in muted grace,
Echo laughter in this place.

Beneath the boughs, where secrets lie,
Gentle breezes brush the sky.
The air is filled with magic's balm,
In the glen, the spirit's calm.

Twilight dances on the brook,
In every nook, nature's book.
Guided by the stars above,
Hearts find peace, and spirits love.

Follow the path where shadows play,
Let them lead you, come what may.
In enchanted lands, lose all fear,
The whispers of the night draw near.

A Canvas of Dappled Light

Sunbeams filter through the leaves,
Painting shadows, nature weaves.
A canvas vast, a gentle sight,
Dappled shades in golden light.

Each color sings in vibrant hues,
A dance performed by morning's muse.
Turning leaves, a fleeting glance,
Invite the heart to join the dance.

Under branches, dreams awake,
A tapestry that nature makes.
With every breeze, a soft embrace,
In this moment, find your place.

Time drips slow amidst the trees,
Whispers echo in the breeze.
Nature's art, a masterpiece,
In quiet moments found in peace.

Every ray a story told,
In dappled light, the world unfolds.
Let your spirit take its flight,
In the magic of the light.

Nature's Untold Stories

In the stillness of the night,
Nature breathes, a gentle sight.
Under stars, the tales unfold,
Whispers of the earth, retold.

A rustling leaf, a soft refrain,
Carrying secrets of joy and pain.
Each creature sings a silent song,
In the wild, where we belong.

Mountains rise with ancient grace,
Holding stories in their place.
Rivers carve through time and stone,
Chronicles of life, alone.

Blossoms bloom, then fade away,
Teaching us to seize the day.
In the winds, a message lies,
Nature's truths beneath the skies.

Gather close, and let it be,
The beauty of eternity.
In every heartbeat, every breath,
Nature tells its tale of death.

A Symphony of Stillness

In quiet corners, whispers breathe,
The gentle rustle of layered leaves.
Moonlight dances, shadows play,
Harmonies of night softly sway.

Crickets sing their midnight song,
Each note a thread where dreams belong.
Stars above, a shimmering choir,
In darkness deep, hearts lift higher.

Stillness wraps the world in grace,
Time slows down, a warm embrace.
Nature breathes a sacred tune,
Under the watch of the glowing moon.

Each heartbeat echoes through the night,
Guided by wisdom, pure and bright.
In this moment, we are one,
In a symphony that can't be undone.

Let the silence fill your soul,
In stillness, we feel truly whole.
This harmony we shall not trade,
For in the quiet, dreams are made.

Secrets Lurking Amongst the Trees

In the woodland's depths, secrets hide,
Whispers float on the evening tide.
Ancient bark holds stories untold,
In the embrace of the green and gold.

Mossy floors beneath our feet,
Where shadows and sunbeams gently meet.
Branches sway with a knowing glance,
Inviting us to join the dance.

Rustling leaves reveal a tale,
Of hidden paths and winds that wail.
The spirits linger, soft and near,
In the forest's heart, they draw us here.

Echoes of laughter, soft and sweet,
Resound in places where spirits greet.
The breeze carries the sound of glee,
In the woods, forever free.

Secrets linger, call us near,
Among the trees, we lose our fear.
In nature's arms, we find our way,
Lost in the magic of the day.

Murmurs of the Forgotten Grove

Amidst the shadows, voices sigh,
Tales of time that flutter by.
In the grove where memories lay,
Soft whispers beckon, come and play.

Worn stones tell of paths once tread,
By those who wandered, lived, and fled.
Beneath the branches, stories weave,
Of love, of loss, in silence grieve.

Faded echoes on the breeze,
Sing softly through the sturdy trees.
The murmurs rise like smoke and fade,
In the twilight's subtle shade.

Time slips through like grains of sand,
In this quiet, sacred land.
We listen close to tales of yore,
In the grove, we yearn for more.

Here lies a treasure, hearts can find,
In forgotten corners, sweet and kind.
The whispers linger, softly swell,
In the grove where secrets dwell.

Solitude's Embrace

In the stillness, shadows blend,
A quiet pause, where sorrows mend.
Wrapped in solitude's gentle shroud,
I walk alone, yet feel so proud.

Golden sun paints the morning sky,
Each breath a reason to question why.
In the hush, my thoughts take flight,
As day unfolds, I find my light.

Whispers of the heart ignite,
In solitude, I find my sight.
A peaceful space, a sacred shore,
Where echoes resonate, forevermore.

Though silence may seem stark and bare,
It cradles hopes beyond compare.
In this embrace, I feel whole,
Solitude sings to my wandering soul.

From shadows deep, new dreams arise,
In quiet moments, I find the prize.
For in this stillness, truth takes form,
In solitude's embrace, I am reborn.

Twilight Secrets of the Timberlands

In twilight's grasp, shadows dance,
Secrets whisper through each branch.
Moonlit paths weave in and out,
Nature's song, a gentle shout.

Stars ignite the sky's deep hue,
The forest breathes, both wild and true.
Stories hidden in the night,
Await the dawn's renewing light.

Mysteries in the rustling leaves,
Softly sighing as night deceives.
A chorus of life, hidden, shy,
Underneath the watchful eye.

Footsteps tread on earthen trails,
Echoes of the wind's faint wails.
Every creature finds its way,
In the twilight's soft ballet.

The timberlands hold secrets deep,
In every nook where shadows creep.
Embrace the silence, breathe it in,
Where dusk and dreams begin to spin.

Dappled Light on the Forest Floor

Sunlight filters through the trees,
Kissing leaves and stirring bees.
Patterns shift upon the ground,
Nature's quilt, profound, unbound.

Ferns unfurl in emerald green,
A tapestry, serene, unseen.
Moss carpets stones in velvety grace,
Gentle whispers fill the space.

Tiny creatures flit about,
Life unfolds without a doubt.
Every ray a story told,
In dappled light, both soft and bold.

Birds above in song ascend,
In this realm where moments blend.
Time stands still, a fleeting lore,
In the dance of light, we explore.

Beneath the canopy, peace resides,
In the forest, life abides.
Awake to wonders, open your eyes,
Where dappled light and beauty lies.

Soft Breath of the Silent Thicket

In thickets dense, the stillness hums,
A soft breath from where nature comes.
Secrets held in foliage tight,
Whispers weave through the fading light.

Petals drift on the evening air,
A world alive, serene and rare.
Every rustle, a calling sigh,
In the silence, life's lullaby.

A rabbit darts, then hides from view,
Underneath the branches' dew.
Nature's heart beats slow and low,
In the thicket, where wild things grow.

And shadows stretch, reaching wide,
In the depths where dreams abide.
Watch the stars begin to peep,
While the forest falls to sleep.

In the thicket, peace takes flight,
Guided by the veil of night.
Take a breath, let stillness creep,
In the soft breath, find your keep.

Ferns Swaying to the Gentle Breeze

Ferns swaying with grace, so light,
Dance in rhythm, pure delight.
Whispers of wind in every frond,
Nature's symphony, sweet and fond.

Beneath the canopy's embrace,
Life unfolds at its own pace.
Every leaf tells tales it knows,
In the breeze, the forest flows.

Sunlight dapples through the shade,
A gentle touch, a bright cascade.
In the hush, the world concedes,
To the sway of emerald reeds.

With every gust, they twist and play,
In harmony, they find their way.
The soft breath of the earth sings on,
A soothing ballad till the dawn.

In this realm where wild hearts roam,
Ferns sway, weaving nature's home.
Join the dance, let worries cease,
In the gentle breeze, find peace.

Reverence in the Shade of Time

In the silence, echoes dwell,
Whispers of ages, stories to tell.
Underneath branches, shadows loom,
Life's secrets held within the bloom.

Leaves tremble with a gentle grace,
Each passing moment leaves a trace.
Time drips like honey, slow and sweet,
In this haven, memories meet.

Nature's breath, a timeless sigh,
Beneath the vast, unending sky.
The heart listens, pulses align,
In reverence for what's divine.

Soft sunlight filters through the green,
In this sanctuary, peace is gleaned.
The world fades, a distant hum,
In the shade, eternity will come.

Time lingers softly in this space,
Holding each moment with tender grace.
Within the stillness, wisdom thrives,
In the shade of time, our spirit survives.

Quietude Lost Among the Cedars

Among the towering cedars, I roam,
Seeking solace, a fleeting home.
The world beyond drifts far away,
In whispers of wind, I wish to stay.

Moss carpets the earth, velvety soft,
Cedar trunks rise, reaching aloft.
In each sigh of the trees, I find
A tranquil heart, a restless mind.

Stillness weaves its gentle thread,
Where secrets of ages quietly spread.
Nature's tapestry, richly spun,
In the shadows, light has begun.

Birds chirp sweetly, their songs unbound,
Echoing echoes of a peaceful sound.
Yet, amidst the calm, I feel a pull,
A longing, a lost quietude's lull.

In the embrace of cedar's shade,
I ponder dreams and plans I made.
Yet here I stand, the present calls,
In this stillness, my spirit enthralls.

As twilight descends, shadows grow,
Stars awaken with a gentle glow.
Though quietude fades, I'll carry near,
The peace found among these cedar spheres.

Embracing Shadows of the Evergreen

Beneath the evergreens, shadows dance,
Life unfolds in a timeless trance.
Each needle's whisper, a story shared,
In the heart of green, our souls laid bare.

Sunlight filters through, a dappled sight,
Creating patterns of gold and light.
In the embrace of the towering trees,
Nature's rhythm flows with ease.

The air is rich, with scents so pure,
An anchor in chaos, a balm for sure.
With every breath, the spirit lifts,
In shadows deep, the heart sifts.

Branches sway, a gentle sigh,
Inviting dreams to wander by.
In this realm, I lose all thought,
Embracing the peace that nature sought.

As evening falls, a cloak descends,
The world slows down, its pulse now bends.
In the depths of green, I find my grace,
In evergreen shadows, I find my place.

Each moment savored, tenderly held,
In the arms of nature, I am compelled.
Together with shadows, I learn to be,
More than a glimpse, I find the key.

Solace of the Secluded Panorama

In a hidden vale, solace thrives,
Where the gentle wind softly dives.
Mountains stand guard, a noble sight,
Wrapping peace in their arms, so tight.

Rivers murmur tales to the stones,
In their cadence, I find my own.
Sunset drapes the world in gold,
Whispers of warmth in the twilight cold.

Each step forward, a journey new,
In this panorama, my heart flies true.
With every breeze, worries release,
In nature's arms, I find my peace.

The sky blushes as dusk draws near,
In the stillness, I shed my fear.
Stars twinkle softly, a canvas bright,
Guiding my thoughts through the velvet night.

In shadows deep, my spirit sings,
Of hidden dreams and gentle wings.
In solitude, the heart learns to soar,
Embracing the solace, forevermore.

So here I stand, in the silent glow,
Among the echoes of earth below.
In the secluded panorama, I find,
The solace of a tranquil mind.

Whispers in the Canopy

Soft murmurs weave through the air,
Leaves dance with stories rare.
Sunlight filters, golden rays,
Nature sings in endless ways.

Chirping echoes fill the space,
Creatures find their rightful place.
Gentle rustles, a secret call,
In the green, we feel it all.

Branches sway, a soothing balm,
The forest breathes, it feels so calm.
With every breeze, a tale unfolds,
In the canopy, magic beholds.

Hidden paths beneath the trees,
Whispers float on summer's breeze.
Memories linger, soft and sweet,
In this world, we find our beat.

Time slows down, we breathe it in,
A symphony where dreams begin.
Whispers weave through every glance,
In nature's arms, we find our dance.

Shadows of the Forgotten Glade

In the glade where shadows play,
Silent echoes drift away.
Mossy stones, a hushed embrace,
Time stands still in this sacred place.

Mysterious whispers haunt the night,
Flickering stars lend their light.
Lost stories linger in the air,
Ancient secrets woven with care.

Each rustling leaf tells of yore,
Of dreams that were, and dreams that soar.
In the dark, memories gleam,
Fleeting glimpses of a dream.

Silent shadows gently sway,
Guiding hearts along the way.
In this realm of twilight hues,
The forgotten glade softly imbues.

We wander through the twilight mist,
With every shadow, a gentle twist.
In the silence, we find our way,
In the glade where shadows play.

Echoes Beneath the Ancient Pines

Beneath the pines, where stillness reigns,
Time whispers softly, avoiding chains.
Echoes linger, a haunting tune,
Beneath the majestic, half-lit moon.

Crickets chirp in harmony,
Nature's symphony, wild and free.
The scent of earth fills the air,
In this quiet, we share our care.

Branches sway in gentle grace,
Guardians of this sacred space.
In their shade, we pause and see,
The beauty of life's mystery.

Soft winds carry stories near,
Every whisper, every tear.
In the silence, wisdom grows,
Under pines, our spirit knows.

Echoes call from days of old,
In every heart, their tales unfold.
Beneath the ancient, wise and tall,
In their presence, we feel it all.

Stillness of the Leafy Veil

In the depths of the leafy veil,
Where secrets rest and dreams set sail.
Sunlight dapples through the green,
A dance of shadows, soft and serene.

Gentle breezes kiss the leaves,
Nature's lullaby, the heart believes.
Whispers float on a fragrant breath,
In this stillness, we confront death.

Each rustle bears a sacred grace,
In the stillness, we find our place.
With every heartbeat, we reconnect,
To the earth, our souls reflect.

Mornings greet with dawn's embrace,
Awakening life in this sacred space.
The leafy veil, a comforting shroud,
In its presence, we feel proud.

Through this stillness, we become,
A part of nature's gentle drum.
In the leafy veil's embrace,
We discover hope in every trace.

Enchanted Stillness in the Trees

Beneath the boughs, the shadows play,
A gentle breeze whispers the day.
Sunlight dapples on the ground,
In this haven, peace is found.

Birds sing softly in the morn,
Nature's beauty, unadorned.
Leaves shimmer with a golden hue,
A tranquil world, serene and true.

Moss carpets roots, so lush and green,
Here, the silence speaks unseen.
Time stands still in this embrace,
A sacred, gentle, timeless space.

Crickets chirp as daylight fades,
The evening's calm, in twilight's shades.
Stars emerge, a diamond quilt,
In this stillness, hearts are built.

Moonlight bathes the forest floor,
In the quiet, spirits soar.
Nature's lullaby, a sweet refrain,
In the trees, we breathe again.

Whispers Amongst the Twisting Vines

Tangled paths weave through the green,
With secrets hidden, yet unseen.
Vines embrace each ancient tree,
In this dance of mystery.

Softly, the shadows intertwine,
As whispers linger, clear and fine.
Fragrant blooms in colors bright,
Guide the way through fading light.

Beneath the arch of leafy lace,
A world unfolds at its own pace.
Every twist a tale to tell,
In hushed tones, they weave the spell.

A symphony of rustling leaves,
In harmony, the forest weaves.
Nature's breath so sweetly sighs,
Amongst the vines, where magic lies.

Night descends with a velvet shroud,
The wilderness moves, alive and proud.
In the dark, soft echoes rise,
Whispers of the wise and old skies.

Mysteries in the Elderwood

In the heart of the forest deep,
Ancient secrets quietly sleep.
The elder trees stand tall and wise,
Guardians of whispers and sighs.

Branches twist like knotted thoughts,
In every shadow, wonder's caught.
Mossy patches cradle dreams,
In the silence, magic seems.

Footsteps echo on the soft earth,
Celebrating the woods' rebirth.
Every sigh holds history's thread,
In the roots where spirits tread.

Moonlight filters through the leaves,
Granting grace to what believes.
Glimmers of fate in every glance,
In the woods, we weave our dance.

By twilight's grace, the stars awake,
In the stillness, our hearts quake.
Mysteries in every shade,
In elderwood, our dreams are laid.

Serenity of the Moss-Laden Stones

Rocks embrace the gentle moss,
In quiet corners, no need for gloss.
Time lingers where the worlds collide,
In nature's arms, we seek to hide.

Each stone holds a tale of yore,
Soft whispers of the earth's core.
Green carpets underfoot reside,
Inviting all to sit and bide.

Water trickles through stony beds,
Life awakens where quiet treads.
Fragments of light dance on the stream,
Beneath the canopy, like a dream.

Morning dew on zephyr's breath,
In moments rich, we ponder death.
Yet in each stone, a story thrives,
In stillness, the spirit survives.

As dusk brings its velvet night,
Stars twinkle with a soft delight.
Serenading stones beneath the moon,
In their calm, we find our tune.

Milton Keynes UK
Ingram Content Group UK Ltd.
UKHW010229111224
452348UK00011B/628